INTRODUCTION

So you want to play drums...so now what?

Congratulations! You've chosen a great instrument—a loud one, but a great one. Whether you own a complete drumset or just a pair of sticks, you're on the right path with this book. And the cool thing is that you'll be ahead of the competition, since many drummers don't know how to read music.

In just a couple of weeks, we'll have you playing some great beats and styles, as well as learning more about your role as a drummer. By the end of this book, you'll be ready to play with a band and play the hits—the Beatles, Clapton, Hendrix, and more—in the FastTrack songbooks.

All we ask is that you observe the three Ps: **patience**, **practice** and **pace yourself**.

Don't try to bite off more than you can chew, and DON'T skip ahead. If your hands hurt, take the day off. If you get frustrated, put the book away and come back later. If you forget something, go back and learn it again. If you're having a great time, keep on playing. Most importantly, have fun.

ABOUT THE AUDIO & VIDEO

Glad you noticed the bonus material – audio tracks and video lessons! Each music example has been recorded so you can hear how it sounds and play along when you're ready. The examples are preceded by a one-measure count-off to indicate tempo and meter. Hal Leonard's **PLAYBACK+** allows you to emphasize the drum part by panning right, or the accompaniment by panning left. This symbol will indicate an audio track is available for the example: 🔊

Select lessons and examples include video lessons, presented by a professional music educator. This symbol will indicate a video lesson is available for the topic or example: ▶

> To access audio and video visit:
> **www.halleonard.com/mylibrary**
>
> Enter Code
> 7113-1022-8150-8231

ISBN 978-1-5400-2205-9

HAL•LEONARD®
7777 W. BLUEMOUND RD. P.O. BOX 13819 MILWAUKEE, WI 53213

Visit Hal Leonard Online at
www.halleonard.com

▶ A GOOD PLACE TO START

Attention "Air Drummers": If you don't have a drumset nearby, no problem. You'll find special notes throughout the book whenever you see this symbol.

Survey your surroundings...

Have a seat and take a look around your set. The drums and cymbals should be arranged in a similar layout to the illustration below:

Tom-toms

Crash cymbal

Ride cymbal

Hi-hat

Snare drum

Bass drum

Air drummers: Try arranging some pots and pans, plastic bowls, or pillows in a similar layout around you.

Sitting at your kit

Make sure your stool isn't too high or too low. You should be able to see over the drums, but you shouldn't be taller than the cymbals.

Straddle the snare drum. Place your right foot on the bass drum pedal and your left foot on the hi-hat pedal.

 Air drummers: Sit on a chair or stool with both feet flat on the floor...prepare to tap.

Holding the sticks

Drummers go through a ton of sticks. For now, though, you should have a pair that's light, durable, and (most of all) comfortable. There are two basic ways to hold your sticks...

matched grip

traditional grip

Only the left hand is different. Most players these days use the **matched grip**, but if you learned **traditional grip** in the school band, go ahead and use traditional.

A FEW MORE THINGS

(...before we jam!)

Parts is parts...

All parts of the sticks, drums and cymbals are used when playing. Take a minute to learn the parts of each, so you'll know exactly where we're talking about later.

Stick

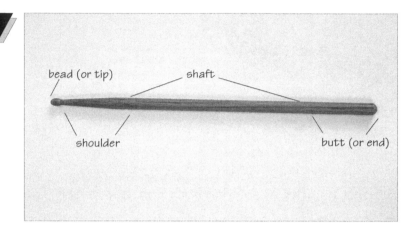

bead (or tip)
shaft
shoulder
butt (or end)

Drumhead

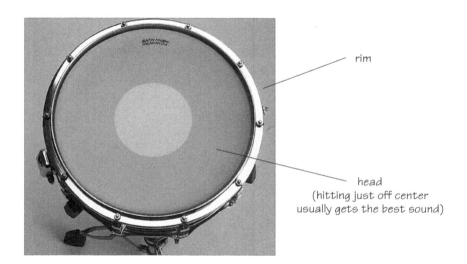

rim

head
(hitting just off center usually gets the best sound)

Cymbal

bell

shoulder

edge

As a drummer, your most important job (besides looking good) is to keep a steady, accurate, and appropriate **tempo**. Tempo means the "speed" at which the music is played.

Keeping time

A **metronome** is a device that keeps perfect time—music time, that is. You simply dial up the number of **beats per minute,** and the metronome begins clicking the beat. Tap your foot in sync with the click, and you're ready to groove...

There are two types of metronomes:

Electronic: These provide a "quiet" option where a light blinks the beat in addition to (or instead of) an audible click. Also cool is that most have an earphone jack, so you can listen to the tempo while you're playing.

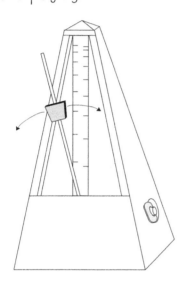

Weighted: These are nice because they look good and don't need batteries. They're very accurate, too, but there's no way to "quiet" the click.

At some point, you owe it to yourself (and the band) to purchase a metronome. They're as essential as a pair of sticks!

Much of the music you play will have **tempo indications**, telling you an approximate speed to play. This can be told four different ways:

 English words ("Fast," "Slow," "Moderate")—Play it like it sounds.

 Foreign words ("Allegro," "Adagio," "Moderato")—Simply look up the word in an inexpensive book of musical terms, such as the *Hal Leonard Pocket Music Dictionary.*

 Metronome markings (♩ = 60, ♩ = 120)—Dial it up on your new metronome.

 All of the above — Just so there's absolutely no misunderstanding!

"DOG-EAR" THESE TWO PAGES!
(... you'll need to review them later!)

▶ Music notation basics

Music is a language with its own symbols, structure, rules (and exceptions to those rules). To write, read and play music requires knowing all the symbols and rules. But let's take it one step at a time (a few now, a few later)...

Notes and rests

Music is written with symbols called **notes** and **rests**, which come in all shapes and sizes. A note means "play;" a rest means "rest" (or "pause"):

whole note
(four beats)

half note
(two beats)

quarter note
(one beat)

whole rest
(pause four beats)

half rest
(pause two beats)

quarter rest
(pause one beat)

Most commonly, a quarter equals one beat. After that, it's just like fractions:

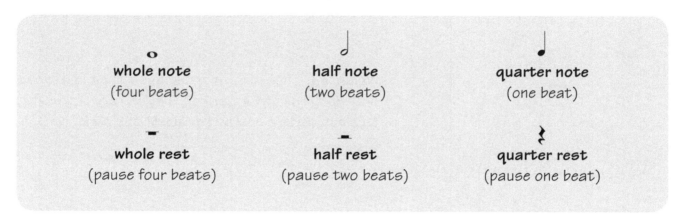

two quarters equal one half
(two beats)

two halves equal one whole
(four beats)

four quarters equal one whole
(four beats)

Staff and Clef

All the notes and rests are written on (or nearby) a **staff,** which consists of five parallel lines and four spaces. For drummers, each represents a different piece of your drumset:

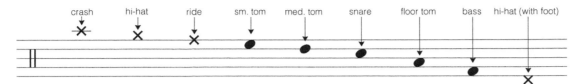

Pitched instruments (such as guitars and keyboards) use the same staff, but the lines and spaces represent different musical tones. A symbol called a **percussion clef** tells you that this is a staff for drum music, not for musical tones.

clef

Don't try to memorize the lines and spaces yet…you'll learn each one as we go through the book.

Measures (or Bars)

Notes on a staff are divided into **measures** (or "bars") to help you keep track of where you are in the song.

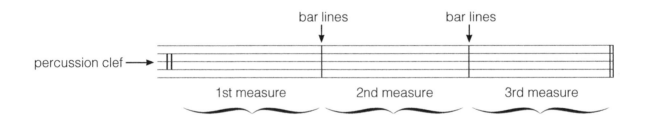

Time signatures (or Meters)

A **time signature** (or "meter") indicates how many beats will appear in each measure. It contains two numbers: the top number tells you how many beats will be in each measure; the bottom number says what type of note will equal one beat.

four beats per measure
quarter note (1/4) = one beat

three beats per measure
quarter note (1/4) = one beat

Relax for a while, read through it again later, and then move on.
(Trust us — as we go through the book, you'll start to understand it.)

LESSON 1
It's time to play something!

You're eager to play, so let's get down to business! We'll start at the top...

 Ride Cymbal

It's called a **ride cymbal** because you "ride" on it. That is, you maintain a steady pattern...

Ride cymbal beats are written on the **top line** of the staff, stem up:

X MARKS THE SPOT: To distinguish from drums, cymbals are written with "x" noteheads. However, if the rhythmic value is a half note or whole note, then a **diamond** notehead will be used (but these are rare).

The ride cymbal can be played several ways. Listen on the audio:

TRACK 1

Play with the bead of the stick.

Play with the bead of the stick on the bell of the ride for a "bell" sound.

Play with the shoulder of the stick on the bell of the ride for a "heavy metal" sound.

Let's get more acquainted with the ride. Count out loud "1, 2, 3, 4" as you play the following with your right hand:

TRACK 2   Hit It!

Can you spare a quarter? How 'bout an eighth?

An **eighth note** has a flag on it:

Two eighth notes equal one quarter note (or one beat). To make it easier on the eyes, eighth notes are connected with a beam:

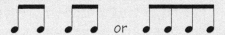

Count eighths by dividing the beat and using the word "and" ("1 &, 2 &, 3 &, 4 &"):

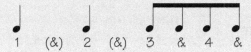

1   (&)   2   (&)   3   &   4   &

NOTE: When counting eighths, the numbers are considered the **downbeats,** while the "ands" are the **upbeats**.

Listen to track 3 before attempting to play eighths:

Ride This! #1
TRACK 3

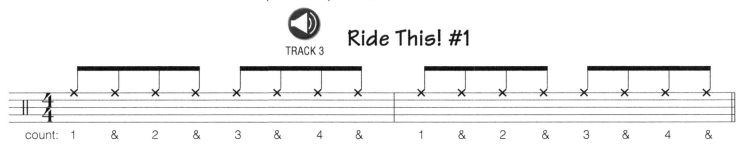

count: 1   &   2   &   3   &   4   &   1   &   2   &   3   &   4   &

Quarter notes often sound good when played on the bell of the ride. Eighth notes often sound better when played on the shoulder of the cymbal. Listen and compare...

Ride This! #2
TRACK 4

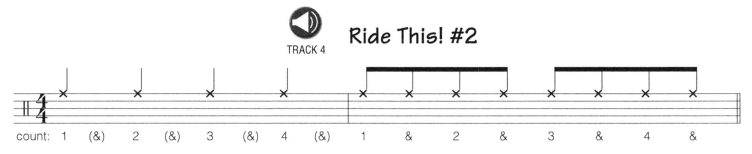

count: 1   (&)   2   (&)   3   (&)   4   (&)   1   &   2   &   3   &   4   &

With many songs you'll play either a quarter ride or an eighth ride. But sometimes you'll play both in the same song to signal differing sections. Practice this so you can switch rhythms without speeding up or slowing down.

Ride This! #3
TRACK 5

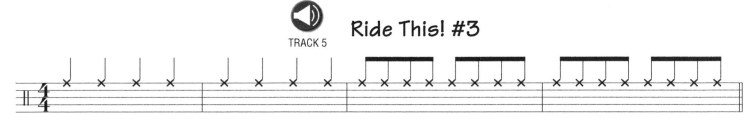

NOTE: Playing eighth notes does not mean playing faster. The tempo stays the same— there are simply twice as many notes per beat!

LESSON 2
Back (to the) beat...

Snare Drum

This is one of the "work horses" of the set. It works in conjunction with the bass drum, sometimes alternating beats with the bass and sometimes playing right along.

Snare drum beats are written on the third space of the staff, stem up or down:

IMPORTANT: Make sure the snare isn't too low. Your forearm should not hit your thigh when you play it.

More options...

There are a several ways to hit the snare. Here are two: **straight shot** and **rimshot**.

STRAIGHT SHOT: Hit the head of the drum with the bead of the stick. Let the stick rebound off the drumhead to allow the drum to vibrate and make a fuller sound.

TRACK 6a

RIMSHOT: Hit the head and rim of the drum (at the same time) with the stick **flat**, but don't let the stick bounce back.

TRACK 6b

Listen to both and then try playing them.

Air drummers: Never mind the rimshot.
Practice playing a steady beat with your right and left hands.

Put it to good use...

Most commonly, the snare accents beats 2 and 4 (also known as the **backbeats**). Count out loud "1, 2, 3, 4" and use your left hand to try out the backbeats:

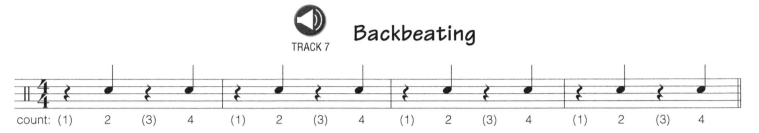

Backbeating
TRACK 7

count: (1) 2 (3) 4 (1) 2 (3) 4 (1) 2 (3) 4 (1) 2 (3) 4

IMPORTANT: A rest does not mean put your hands down or rest your feet! During a rest, you should read ahead and ready your hands and feet for the next set of beats.

Play the cymbal and snare drum together on the next four examples, which are recorded back to back on the same track:

Snare/Ride
TRACK 8

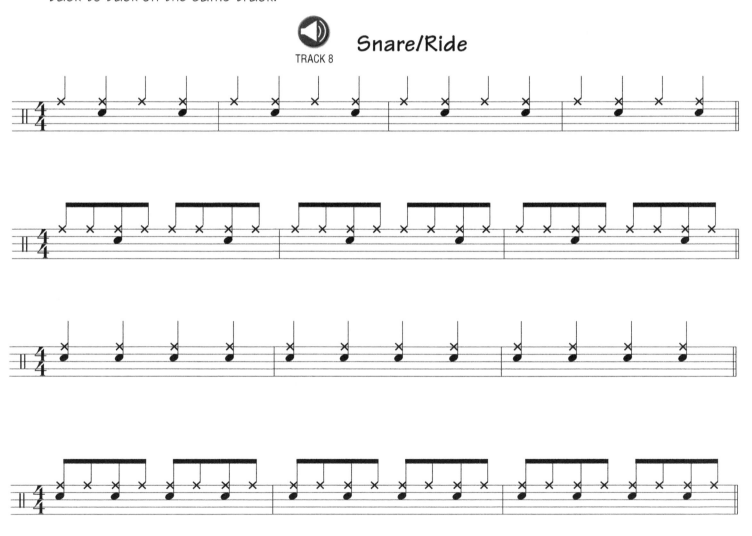

☞ This is a good time to take a break. When you come back, review Lessons 1 and 2 before moving to Lesson 3.

LESSON 3
Feet keep the beat...

Welcome back! Put down your sticks, keep resting those hands, and let's concentrate on your feet.

 Bass Drum

The **bass drum** is another "work horse" of your set—it is rarely quiet. Its primary function is to accent the main beats of the song, usually beats 1 and 3.

Bass drum beats are written on the lowest space of the staff with the stem down.

The bass drum is played by pushing the pedal with your right foot. The harder you push, the louder it sounds. Try it!

You can pedal two ways:

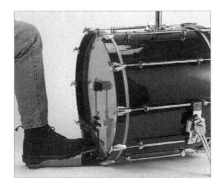

foot flat on pedal

heel off the pedal

With your foot flat on the pedal, simply move your ankle up and down. With your heel off the pedal, it's necessary to use your whole leg to keep a steady beat going.

 Air drummers: Simulate this by tapping your foot up and down normally and then stomping with the whole leg.

Put it to more good use!

Let's get better acquainted with the bass drum with some examples. Remember to count out loud ("1 &, 2 &, 3 &, 4 &"). The clicks keep going to help out...

TRACK 9 **Feet Beats #1**

count: 1 (& 2 &) 3 (& 4 &)   1 (& 2 & 3 & 4 &)   etc.

Now let's mix in some half rests. Remember to count out loud:

TRACK 10 **Feet Beats #2**

Now add some quarter rests, too:

TRACK 11 **Feet Beats #3**

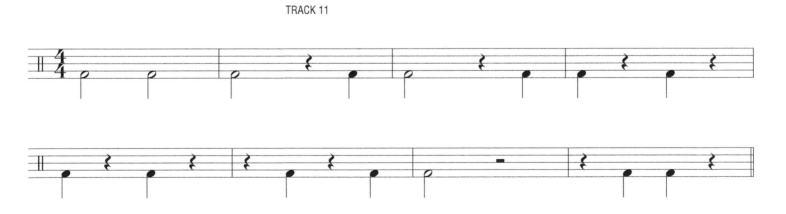

Terrific! But don't stop there...

Add the ride (along with the keyboard player on the tracks):

Now combine the bass and snare (play all snare notes with the left hand):

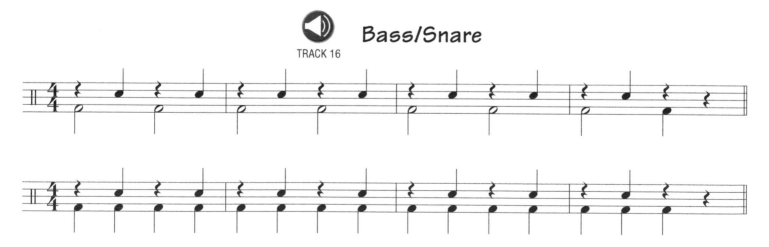

Always practice slowly and try faster tempos only as you become more confident with the rhythms.

LESSON 4
All together now...

▶ Putting it together

The next four beat patterns are simple but effective. They've been used on a **lot** of records by some of the best drummers.

SHORTHAND: This symbol (℅) means to repeat the previous measure. Saves us having to write it out again.

Attitude adjustment...

How you play is as important as (if not more important than) **what** you play. A simple beat played with drive and conviction is more impressive than a complex beat played weak. So, play this page again like the drummer you really are!

LESSON 5

More cymbal symbols...

You know the ride and two very important drums. Let's take a look at two more important cymbals—the **hi-hat**. These can be played several ways: open or closed, with the foot, with the sticks, or all of the above...

 **Hi-Hat Cymbals (with the stick)**

Instead of riding on the ride cymbal, you can ride on the hi-hat with the same hand you used on the ride cymbal (the right one, of course). Simply hold the hi-hat closed (pedal down) with your foot and hit the edge of the cymbals with the shoulder of the stick.

Hi-hat beats that are played with the sticks are written on the top space above the staff, stem up.

Hold the cymbals closed tightly for a crisp sound, or slightly loose for a "sloshy" sound.

Nice Hat #1
TRACK 21

Nice Hat #2
TRACK 22

Nice Hat #3
TRACK 23

Nice Hat #4
TRACK 24

Hi-Hat Cymbals (with the foot)

Play the hi-hat just like the bass drum—with the pedal, either hard or soft. The harder you push, the "crisper" the sound.

Hi-hat beats that are played with the foot are written just below the staff, stem down.

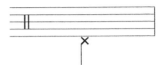

Play the ride cymbal with the right hand and the hi-hat with your left foot.

My Left Foot

TRACK 25

Repeat these examples but faster this time.

Left, Right, Left...

You can put the sticks down again for the next examples—just use your feet!

Feet Beats #4

TRACK 26

All four limbs...

Okay, pick 'em back up (your sticks, that is):

Nimble Limbs #1

TRACK 27

Nimble Limbs #2

TRACK 28

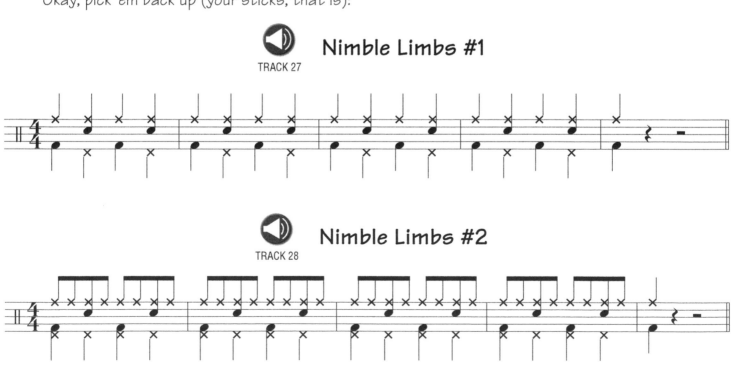

LESSON 6

▶ *Eighth-note grooves*

Time to dig in and start grooving. These eighth-note patterns will help increase both your music-reading skills and your dexterity.

Eighths on the Bass Drum

Use an eighth-note ride and concentrate on playing clean quarters and eighths with the bass drum:

Eighth Ride #1
TRACK 29

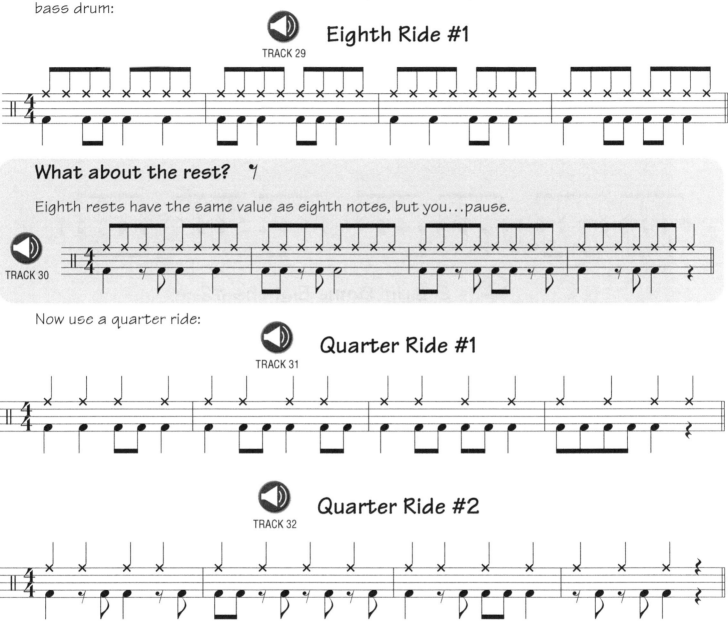

What about the rest? ↄ

Eighth rests have the same value as eighth notes, but you...pause.

TRACK 30

Now use a quarter ride:

Quarter Ride #1
TRACK 31

Quarter Ride #2
TRACK 32

Switch to an eighth ride and add snare drum on the backbeats:

Eighth Ride #2
TRACK 33

Now try backbeats with a quarter-note ride:

Quarter Ride #3

TRACK 34

Eighths on the Snare Drum

Use an eighth ride. Remember to practice slowly and speed up only when you feel more comfortable with the rhythm:

Snarin' Some Eighths #1

TRACK 35

Snarin' Some Eighths #2

TRACK 36

Now add the bass drum:

Full Groove (Eighth Ride)

TRACK 37

Full Groove (Quarter Ride)

TRACK 38

Try this page again but with hi-hat instead of ride cymbal.

20

Repeat signs have two dots before or after a double bar line ( ). They simply tell you to (you guessed it!) repeat everything in between. If only one sign appears ( ), repeat from the beginning of the piece.

TRACK 39

Twelve great grooves...

Here are some terrific one-bar grooves to repeat over and over again. These are not designed to be played one right after another, but on the audio you'll hear each one played twice, immediately followed by the next one...

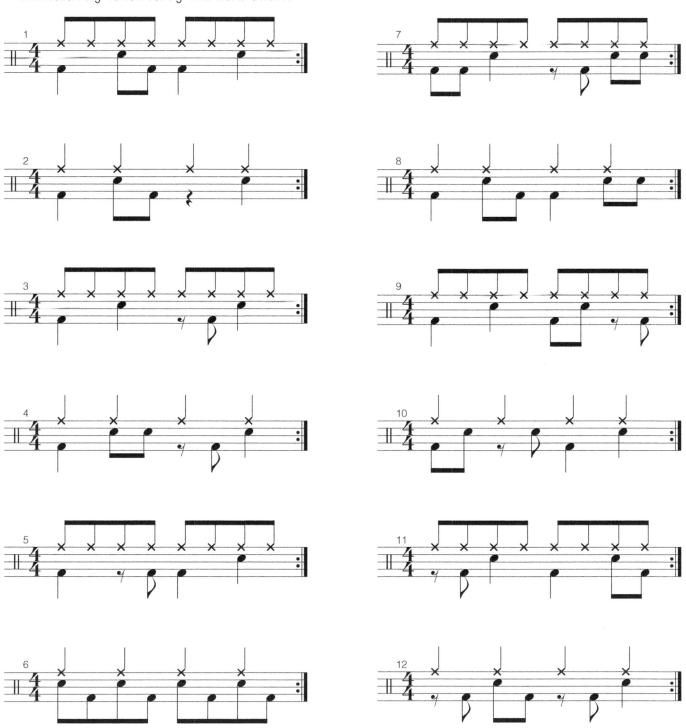

LESSON 7

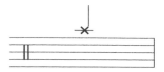 *A crash course in cymbals...*

Crash Cymbal

The **crash cymbal** is used to accentuate a powerful beat, to add more energy to **any** beat, or to mark different sections of the song.

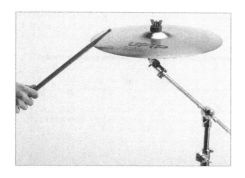

Crash cymbal beats are written on a line above the staff, stem up. This "off the staff" line is called a **ledger line**.

There's really only one good way to play a crash cymbal—LOUD! With the right hand, smack the edge of the crash cymbal with the shoulder or shaft of the stick, using a glancing blow.

Crash This!

TRACK 40

Try to move quickly between the ride and the crash cymbal, so you don't miss even a single eighth note.

Smash and Crash

TRACK 41

Watch the music, **not** your hands! Your brain has enough going on—don't try to memorize the grooves, too!

Sixteenth notes

These have two flags or beams: or

Sixteenth rests look like eighth rests but with two flags: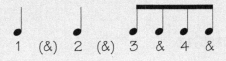

More fractions...

Four sixteenth notes equal one quarter note; two sixteenth notes equal one eighth note. Here's a chart to help you see the relationship of the rhythmic values:

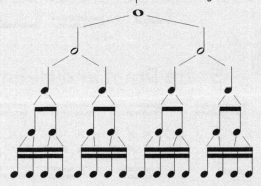

To count sixteenths, divide the beat even further by counting "1 e & a, 2 e & a, 3 e & a, 4 e & a":

Play sixteenths on the ride, while keeping count with the bass and snare:

Goin' on Sixteen

TRACK 42

Try alternating hands to play sixteenths on the hi-hat. The right hand will move quickly to hit the snare on the backbeats.

Alternating Hands

TRACK 43

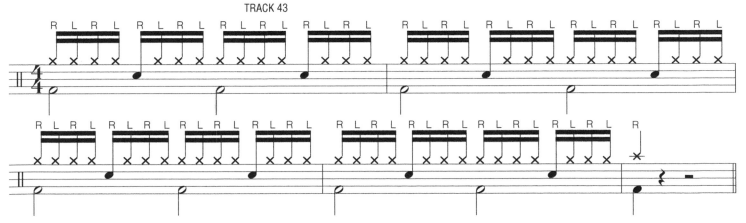

Not so fast, pal!

Didn't think you'd learn 'em **that** quickly, did you? Here are some examples that allow you to learn sixteenths on all the drums and cymbals you know…

Bass Drum and Ride

TRACK 44

Snare Drum and Hi-hat:

TRACK 45

IMPORTANT: Remember to count "1 e & a, 2 e & a, 3 e & a, 4 e & a" so that the bass drum sixteenths are played properly.

Bass Sixteenths

TRACK 46

Snare Sixteenths

TRACK 47

Mix 'em all together…

Mixed Up #1

TRACK 48

Mixed Up #2

TRACK 49

LESSON 8

 Dots...

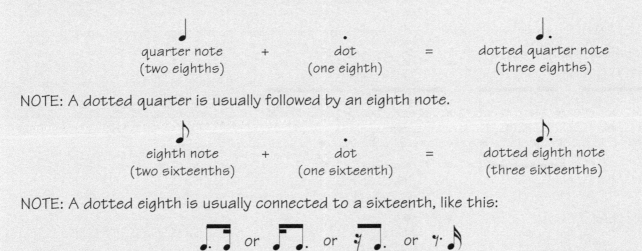

A **dot** extends a note or rest by one-half of its value. For drummers, the two most common are the **dotted quarter** and **dotted eighth**.

| quarter note (two eighths) | + | dot (one eighth) | = | dotted quarter note (three eighths) |

NOTE: A dotted quarter is usually followed by an eighth note.

| eighth note (two sixteenths) | + | dot (one sixteenth) | = | dotted eighth note (three sixteenths) |

NOTE: A dotted eighth is usually connected to a sixteenth, like this:

The following examples employ dotted notes. Practice slowly and count out loud:

Dot This! #1
TRACK 50

Dot This! #2
TRACK 51

Dot This! #3
TRACK 52

Twice the fun...

With many songs, you will play the same one-bar beat over and over. (Remember the one-bar repeat sign on page 15?) But sometimes, it's more interesting to repeat a two-bar pattern.

A **two-measure repeat sign** looks like this:

IMPORTANT: It does not mean you repeat one bar twice; it means to repeat the two previous bars again. For example, when you see this:

...play this:

Audio track 53 will give you a better idea...

TRACK 53 Doubling Up

Snare to spare...

With a lot of drumset playing, each hand will be playing independently on a different part of the beat. Sometimes, though, the hands work together to play rhythms.

Play the following snare drum solo. Maintain a steady bass drum beat and be sure to observe the suggested **sticking** (which hand to use), which is written above the staff.

TRACK 54

Sticking to It #1

☞ Use these rhythms as a basis for fills and solos.

LESSON 9

 *Fills*

You've learned the pieces of your set that provide the basic beats. Now let's jazz it up a bit with three more drums...

Tom-Toms

The sound of your three **tom-toms** (or "toms") ranges from high to low:

Rack toms are mounted on the bass drum. The **small tom** is written on the top space; the **medium tom** is written on the fourth line:

The **floor tom** sits on the floor. It is written on the space above the bass drum:

☞ NOTE: You may have even more toms. For now, just concentrate on these main three.

Play each tom, from high to low, from low to high. Then try this example (but make sure you use the correct sticking)...

 **Sticking to It #2**

TRACK 55

 Air drummers: Get out some more pans, bowls, pillows, siblings...whatever you're hitting.

The toms can be played on the main beats, just like the snare and bass, but more commonly they are used to play fills, like in this groove:

TRACK 56 **Fill This!**

Doing your own thing...

You can use the toms, snare, cymbals, or everything for a fill. Fills can be one beat, two beats, or more. Use sixteenths, eighths, or even quarters. Listen to four different kinds of fills on track 57, then try creating your own:

TRACK 57 **A Fill for All Seasons**

You can use all (or just parts) of the following patterns to create fills. You can even string them together for drum solos. Track 58 plays each pattern twice, followed immediately by the next one.

Getting Around

HELPFUL HINT: Let your eyes read ahead of the note that you're actually playing. That way, you'll know what's coming and ready your hands early.

Not just filling...

Tom-toms can also be incorporated into beats and grooves to add color and power.

Power Toms #1

TRACK 59

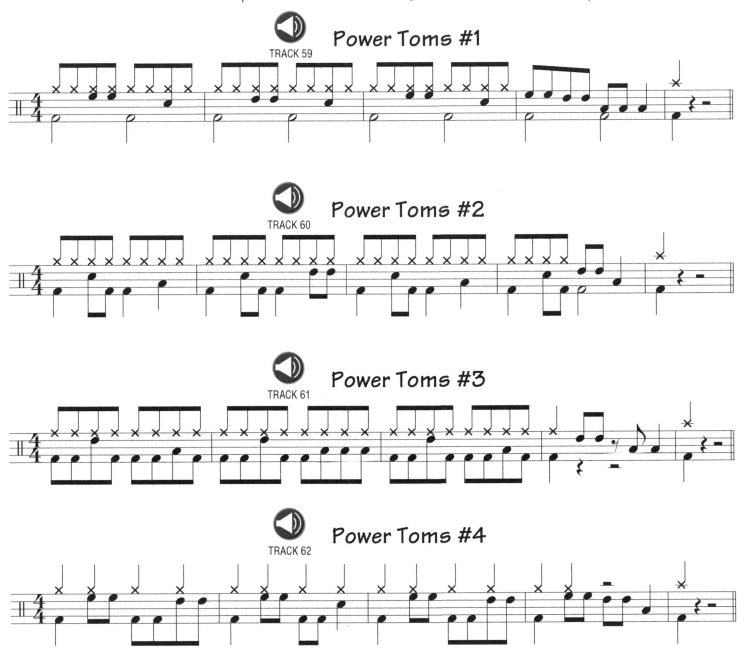

Power Toms #2

TRACK 60

Power Toms #3

TRACK 61

Power Toms #4

TRACK 62

For some real power, ride on the floor tom instead of the hi-hat or ride cymbal.

Ridin' the Toms

TRACK 63

LESSON 10
 *You got style...*

As we mentioned, there are several ways to play many of the pieces in your set...

Open Hi-Hat

When riding on a closed hi-hat, you can add color and punctuation to a beat by opening the hi-hat occasionally. Track 64 gives you a good idea of this new sound.

An open hi-hat note is marked by an "o" (for "open") above the note.

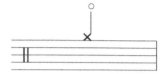

Raise your foot off the pedal as you play the open note by hitting the hi-hat cymbals with your stick, then bring the cymbals back together with the pedal at the same time you strike the next note:

Open Hi-Hat
TRACK 64

raise foot as you play this note   press foot down as you play this one

Now incorporate this style into some beats:

Open-Close #1
TRACK 65

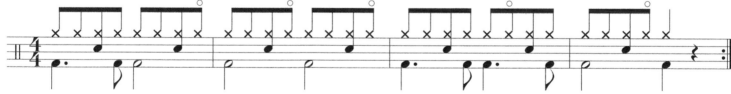

Open-Close #2
TRACK 66

Disco Days
TRACK 67

▶ Cross-Stick Snare Drum

A popular and much-used effect involves laying the stick across the snare drum head and clicking the shoulder of the stick against the rim.

The **cross-stick** sound is notated by a circle around a snare drum note:

Cross-stick is especially useful with ballads...

🔊 Ballad Style #1

TRACK 68

🔊 Ballad Style #2

TRACK 69

Here are two more patterns that use the cross-stick sound:

🔊 Cross My Stick #1

TRACK 70

🔊 Cross My Stick #2

TRACK 71

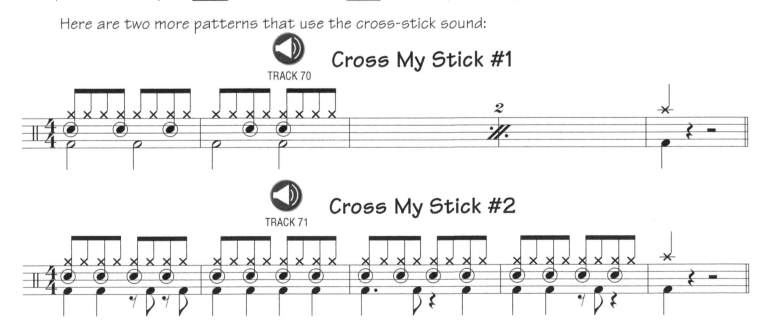

Fantastic! Check the tempo on your metronome. Are you playing up to speed yet?

A great way to make a drum sound bigger and fatter is to hit it with both sticks at ALMOST the same time. This effect is called a **flam**, which looks like this:

The little note is called a **grace note** and is hit just slightly before and slightly softer than the main note. To play a flam, start with one stick just an inch or two above the drum while the other hand readies to hit from the regular (or accent) position. If you bring the sticks down at the same time, the one closest to the drumhead will hit first, producing the "fat" flam sound.

Flams can be played on the same drum, or between different drums. Track 72 gives you an idea of these sounds:

TRACK 72

Flim-Flam-Floom

Flams can be used to give a "military" sound to a snare drum part...

TRACK 73

Battle Flam of the Republic

Flams can also add power to intros, grooves and fills...

TRACK 74

Flam This!

▶ 3/4 METER

Although 4/4 meter is the most common time signature in rock, blues, country, funk, and pop music, it's not the ONLY time signature used. Another time signature that turns up from time to time (pardon the pun!) is 3/4. (Flip back to page 7 for a quick review.)

Below are twelve grooves in 3/4 meter (that is, three beats per measure). Each one is played twice on track 75, followed immediately by the next one…

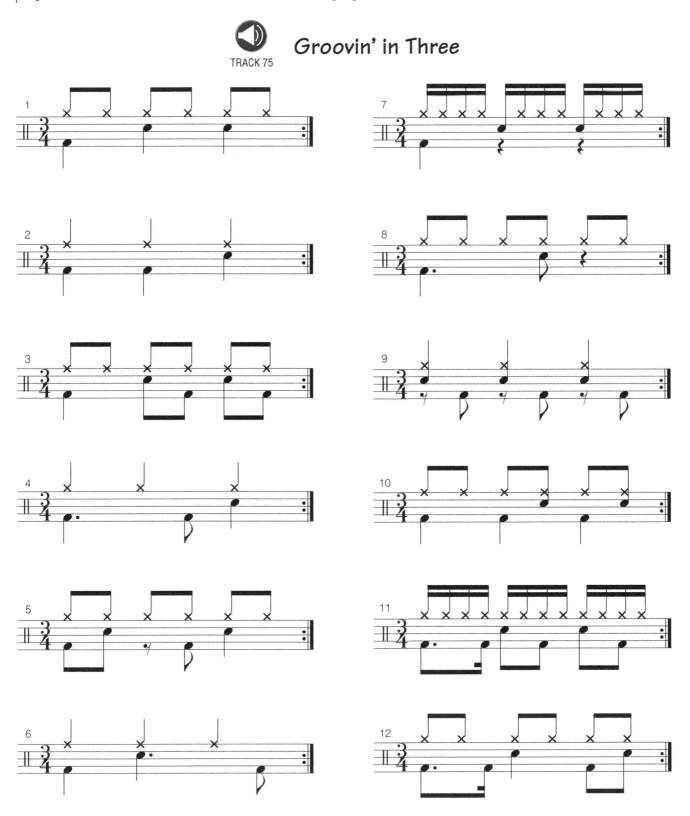

🔊 **Groovin' in Three**

TRACK 75

Try them once more, but faster this time…

LESSON 11

▶ Take it away...

Most of the time, the other instruments will stop playing (maybe even leave the stage!) when it's time for your drum solo. (This really isn't fair, since you don't get a break during THEIR solos!)

When you're the only one playing, the challenge is to keep the groove going and still be able to play musical phrases. One way to pull this off is to maintain a steady pulse on the bass drum and "solo" over that. Try this one on for size...

Fab Solo

TRACK 76

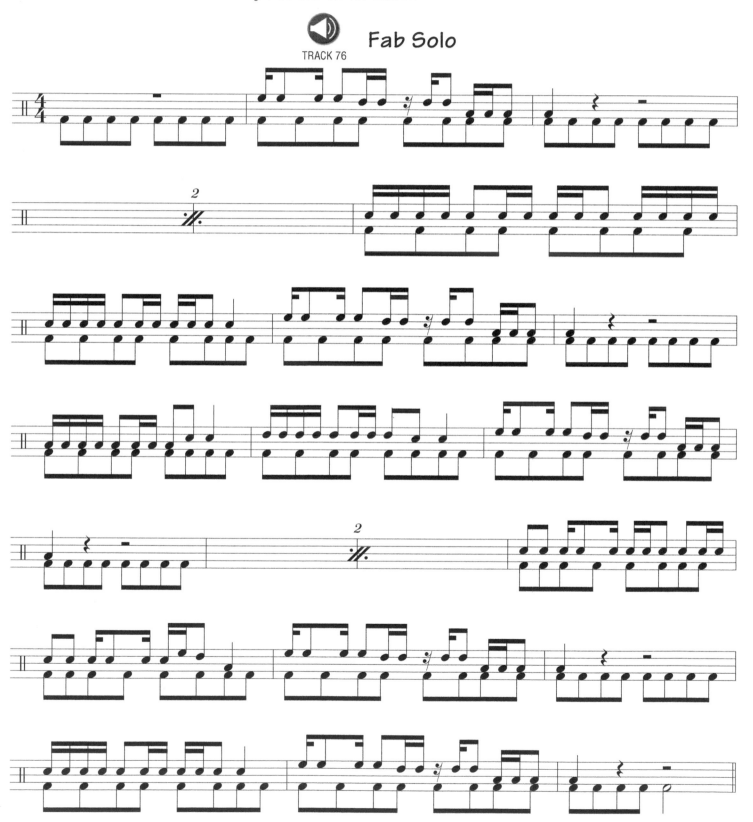

Another way to hold a groove when soloing is to keep a steady flow of sixteenths going and create rhythmic interest by **accenting** certain notes. An accented note is marked with the following sign: >

The following pattern will help you learn to put accents on different parts of the beats. Play the accented notes a lot louder than the unaccented ones.

TRACK 77

Accentuate It!

Now try another solo...

TRACK 78

Accent on Solo

THE JOYS OF TOYS

If you have a standard drumset, we've probably covered most (if not all) of the pieces. However, you may have (or want to add) a few more "toys." Here's a picture of a dream set, labeled with the extras...

More tom-toms
The more the merrier—gives you more choices for improvising fills

More cymbals
Crash away! (Your poor neighbors?!)

Tambourine
On a stand, it becomes another hi-hat substitute

Cowbell
Substitute it for the hi-hat or ride for a harder edge sound

Double bass pedal or **two bass drums**
Either allows you to play faster eighths and sixteenths with your feet

 Air drummers: Don't be jealous—just get more cookware. Seriously, a teapot makes a great cowbell sound!

LESSON 12

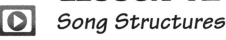

Song Structures

Okay, you can play quarter-note feels, eighth-note feels, and sixteenth-note feels. You can play fills and solos. It's time to start playing songs!

But you can't just throw in any old beat in any old place, and there are very specific times and places for fills and cymbal crashes. Let's take a minute to look at song structure...

Playing Songs

Most songs have different sections, which might include any or all of the following:

 INTRODUCTION (or "intro"): This is a short section at the beginning that "introduces" the song to the listeners.

 VERSES: One of the main sections of the song is the verse. There will usually be several verses, all with the same music but each with different lyrics.

 CHORUS: Another main section of a song is the chorus. Again, there might be several choruses in between the verses, but each chorus will often have the same lyrics.

 BRIDGE: This section makes a transition from one part of a song to the next. For example, you may find a bridge between the chorus and next verse.

 SOLOS: Sometimes solos are played over the verse or chorus structure, but in some songs the solo section has its own structure. The solo sections are usually given to the guitarist, but occasionally you'll get lucky and have the spotlight on you.

 OUTRO: Similar to the "intro," this section brings the song to an end. Without an "outro," the song can end suddenly, or fade out. Any way is fine, as long as it's believable and played with conviction.

What and when...

You will often play the same basic beat throughout the entire song, but sometimes you will make slight variations for each section. Even then, you should probably play each chorus the same, each verse the same, etc. (This will signal the listeners as to the part of the song they are hearing.)

Cymbal crashes are effective for marking the beginning of a new section, or the halfway point of a section.

Fills are most effective when played at the very end of a section. They serve as a signal that the song is about to go into new (perhaps uncharted) territory.

> *G*ot all that? Not sure? Don't worry—the examples on the next few pages
> will give you some better ideas about how to create drum parts for songs.
> At the end you have three complete songs waiting for you... but DON'T SKIP AHEAD!

Make a difference...

As we just explained, you will often play a single beat throughout most of the song, embellishing with various fills and cymbal crashes. Sometimes it's good to change the **sound** and **feel** of the beat you're playing in different sections of the song.

 You might ride on the hi-hat during the verse and switch to the ride cymbal during the choruses, keeping the snare and bass the same.

 You might switch from an eighth-note ride in the verses to a quarter-note ride during the choruses, again keeping the snare and bass the same.

 Try combining a change of sound and feel: quarter-note ride on hi-hat for the verse; eighth-note ride on cymbal during the chorus. And perhaps a quarter-note ride on the bell of the cymbal during the guitar solo.

Sometimes you will want to change the beat altogether between different sections of the song. In most cases, the different beats you use within one song should be fairly close. Check out the next three examples for some ideas:

TRACK 79

Changin' It Up #1

Changin' It Up #2

TRACK 80

Changin' It Up #3

TRACK 81

You are nearing the end of this book.
Run to your local music dealer and get FastTrack Drums Songbook 1!

Endings...

In many cases, the only difference between the two verses or choruses of a song is the **lyrics**. The guitar, bass, keyboard and drums will be playing the exact same thing during each section—except maybe the very end.

Try playing a different fill (or make some kind of change) at the end of each section to lead into the next.

In such cases, you'll see music written with **first and second endings**, indicated by a bracket and the numbers "1" and "2" above the staff. In the example below, play until you reach the repeat sign in line 3, then repeat back to the beginning. The second time through, skip the "1st ending" and play the "2nd ending" through to the end.

Listen to track 82 before playing, and you'll know what we mean...

If at First...

TRACK 82

Anticipation...

Don't give away everything you've got in the first four bars! It is often very effective to start out simple and gradually build your drum part up as the song continues. The audience's excitement should build right along with your playing, as in the following example...

Build It Up!

TRACK 83

HALF-TIME
(... without a marching band)

The same type of beat can be written two different ways. For example, instead of writing a slow ballad groove with a sixteenth ride and snare drum hits on backbeats 2 and 4, the same pattern can be notated with an eighth-note ride and a snare drum hit on beat 3 of each measure.

This is called a **half-time feel**. Listen to track 84. It can be notated either of the ways shown below. If written the first way, the intro clicks on the audio represent four quarter notes; but for the second notation, the clicks represent four half notes.

  It's All the Same

TRACK 84

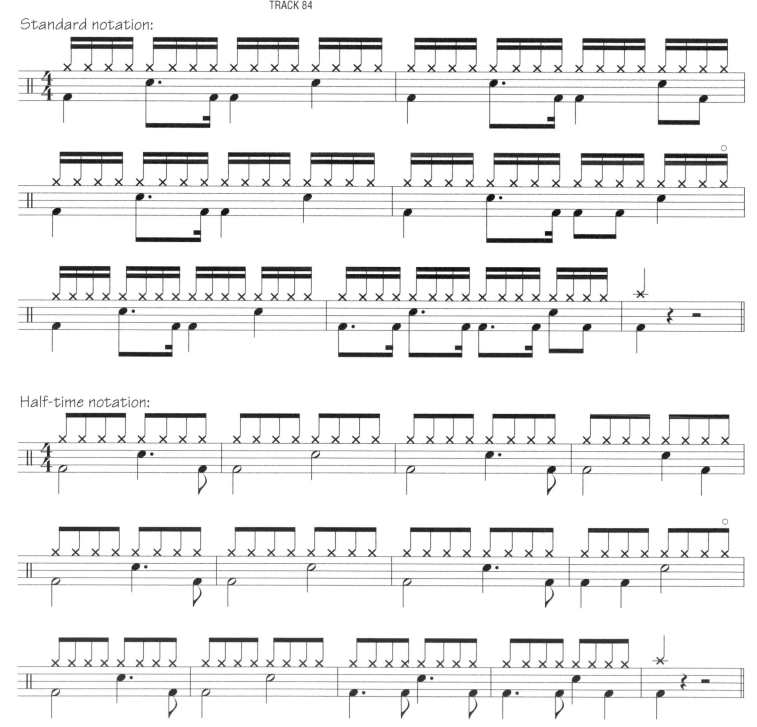

Standard notation:

Half-time notation:

LESSON 13
Time to charge admission...

This isn't really a Lesson... it's a jam session!

All the *FastTrack* books (guitar, keyboard, bass and drums) have the same last section. This way, you can either play by yourself along with the audio or form a band with your friends.

So, whether the band's on the audio or in your garage, let the show begin...

TRACK 85   TRACK 86

full band   minus drums

Exit for Freedom

Unplugged Ballad

Billy B. Badd

TRACK 89
full
band

TRACK 90
minus
drums

Conclusion

Bravo! Encore!!

Remember to practice often and always try to learn more about your instrument.

AUDIO INDEX